Through Oceans - Meer Wege

Miri Dings

BookLeaf
Publishing

India | USA | UK

Cover Bild von Schäferle auf Pixabay

Presentation by *BookLeaf Publishing*

Web: www.bookleafpub.com

E-mail: info@bookleafpub.com

ISBN: 9789357448963

First edition 2022

DEDICATION

for all those who love and life the oceans -
inside and outside

ACKNOWLEDGEMENT

I always love to read this part of a book - the
overwhelming feeling of gratitude and love an
author shares with the people who helped her or
him to bring a book to life. It always touches me
deeply.
So here is my present of love and gratitude to all
those who were a part of this journey - some
may unnamed but still not less important.
Vanessa, you re-opened the door to the world of
poetry for me back then in Lisboa. Without your
inspiration and encouragement this book
wouldn't be the same. Thank you for alway
believing in me.
Unknown but also a big inspiration for starting
to write poems again I have to thank Noor
Unnahar. Yesterday I was the moon was my first
self bought poetry book.
My whole family - for they drive me crazy as
f*ck and are a big part of inspiration while
climbing out of another dark whole they kicked
me in. Whether it is sometimes really hard for
me - I really do love you all very much.
Anna, who showed me that you can get out of
every shit that happened to you and when you do
you'll be the most dazzling and beamy version

of yourself. I would have never come this far without you.

Ramona, you've always been a creative person and shared it with me. I learned from you to talk about my creativity and not be ashamed of it.

Alex, you went in my life and got a big part of it without me even recognizing it. But you were always there and I just begin to realize how precious you are to me. I wouldn't know where I'd ended up without you by my side and therefore I'm forever grateful.

Myself, for never giving up and the imperturbable believe it will all work out just fine some day.

PREFACE

Poetry has had a small but remarkable relevance
and impact in my life. When I was young I
wrote some very gloomy verses with mostly
more odd than beautiful rhymes.
But in the books I've loved so much, I always
read this magical poems that seemed to change
the world or at least explain it in some way.
And as I grew up and writing was still an all
time habit, it happens that I wrote poems again.
Very different from the early beginnings but so
honest and from the very center of my heart, that
I recognized for the first time that it doesn't
depend on the words or their meaning. More on
the feeling between the letters and the motions
that take place inside by reading between the
lines.
So this is me - my very heart and soul - you hold
in hands and you might feel among the black
and white of letters and paper.

ich bin viele
und nur ich

ich bin laute farben und bunte töne.
viele lass mal machen und wird schon gut gehen.
mit dem kopf durch die wand und dem kleinen
zeh im großen teich.

ich bin leise melodien und gedecktes pastell.
viele ich brauche nen moment für mich und ist
grad viel.
mit heißem tee und ner kuscheldecke und mehr
büchern als realität.

ich bin nur noch ein kapitel und songtexte sind
meine muttersprache.
ich bin mit jedem best friends und komm mir
nicht zu nah.

ich bin das rauschen des meeres. sonne und
strand mit salzluft.
ich bin das grün der wiesen. berge und wald mit
blütenpracht.

ich bin einfach, ich bin kompliziert.
ich bin öko, bewusstsein und weltverbesserin.
ich bin bequem, kochfaul und altbewährtes.

ich bin heil und ich habe macken.
ich bin auf dem weg und schon angekommen.

lost self

she lost herself
in other people
again and again.

til she learned
not to drown
but to swim.

and she swam
in the ocean
of herself.

some joined her
some left.

but she never drowned
in others again.

and recognized the
beauty of herself.

as she found
the ocean in herself
to be the answer
to everything.

human things

in a time
which is full of
things
instead of
humans

find the time to
stand still.

take a breath
and let shine your
love
as bright as the
sun

on a summerday.

Hin und Her

Hell. Dunkel. Hell. Dunkel.
Flackern.
Das Gefühl zu erstrahlen. Zu erlöschen.
Flackern.

Vor. Zurück. Vor. Zurück.
Illusion.
Das Gefühl zu erreichen. Zu scheitern.
Illusion.

Bunt. Einfarbig. Bunt. Einfarbig.
Natur.
Das Gefühl zu blühen. Zu verwelken.
Natur.

Sein. Tun. Sein. Tun.
Ich.
Das Gefühl zu fließen. Zu stoppen.
Ich.

Autopilot und Flugmodus

Dinge erledigen.
To Do Listen füllen
- und nicht leeren.

Termine ausmachen.
Zwischen den Gesprächen
- nur hin und her rennen.

Gedanken kreisen.
Immer mit dem Kopf
- irgendwo ohne Ruhe.

Keine Zeit haben.
Kaum Pausen zu nehmen
- um durchzuatmen.

Wie auf Autopilot,
fliegt mein Leben
- einfach an mir vorbei.

Stop! Pause-Taste!
Selbstreflektion.

Wie kann es sein,
dass mein Leben
mich selbst überholt
ohne, dass ich es merke?

Wie kann ich selbst
wieder zur Pilotin
meines Lebens werden,
Ziel und Reise selbstbestimmt?

Die To Do Liste:
beiseite legen.
& den Kopf leeren.

Die Termine:
absagen.
& stehen bleiben.

Die Gedanken:
runterschreiben.
& loslassen.

Wie im Flugmodus:
für andere nicht erreichbar.
& nur für mich sein.

Neustart! Play-Taste!
Eigenverantwortung.

Mein Leben einholen,
indem ich es betrachte,
wenn es stillsteht und
ich bewusst BIN.

Nicht nur für mein Tun,
sondern auch für mein Sein
und Fühlen beachten
und den Raum geben.

Vom Autopilot zum Flugmodus -
& selbst mit dem Leben fliegen,
statt ihm beim Vorbeisegeln zuzusehen.

sunset

she's like the sunset
the last beams
softly touching
your skin

caressing you
so tender
the warmth hugging
your ceek

and disappearing
right after
letting you stand
there in the ocean

your feet in
the shallow water
playing around
your ankles

leaving you
with the promise
to return on
the next day

knowing you'll never
be alone
cause the ocean
is always at
your side

being special

how can you be special?
it's nothing you do.
it's everything you are.

and when you get aware of that
you can decide:

let everything you are influence what you do
and let nothing you do destroy who you are.

so, it's a decision
to be the special you
you naturally are.

we are all a little april sometimes

Die Sonne scheint und es regnet.
Irgendwie mag ich den April.
Fühlen wir uns nicht alle ab und zu wie April?
Gleichzeitig strahlend und regnerisch.

Bekommen wir dafür nicht auch häufig
negatives Feedback.
Obwohl wir uns eigentlich nur Liebe und
Akzeptanz wünschen?
Besonders in diesen Momenten.

So, let's make a difference – because
we are all a little april sometimes.

If you feel like april right now – remember
it's great you are here
you are loved
it's okay to be a little april
give yourself a hug

And do it like april
shine through rain.

love yourself

things we have shall
fill the holes in our souls.
but they don't.

just feelings can fill them
when we find the courage
to look inside.

face our inner monsters
give them a warm hug
and let the love float them.

the love of ourselves.
every day.
every hour.
every minute.

the love to be
what we are.
who we are.
everything we are.

Lotus

They told me to be
thankful
for the mud.

They told me to grow a
Lotus
out of the mud.

But how can I?
It takes the light.
It smells bad.
It is slippery.

But that's just the obvious.
It also gives minerals.
It saves energy.
It is full of air.

You can take the good ones
and grow
into the light
and love
the mud for what it is.

Without this basement
there won't be the
possibility to grow either.

So be
thankful
for the mud.

For it made you
grow to a
Lotus.

What I learned from
my mother

My mother told me
it's ok to be weak.

But she also thought me
to be strong.

So, I learned:
Weakness is a strength.
And –
Strength is a weakness.

It always depends on the situation,
on the decision, you make
and the reason why you take it.

how to follow your
heart

how can you follow your heart
when you don't know what it wants?
when you don't see the direction it's leading?
when you don't feel what is its passion?

only with trust you can follow
the path which will lead you
to your inner self.

the trust that everything will come at the right
time.
that everything happens for a reason.
that you will feel the way when it's there.

and believe
you will have
the courage
to take it.

then you will follow your heart
before even recognizing it and
like you've never done anything else.

Gedanken Meer

Ich denke und denke,
tauche tiefer und tiefer
ein - in ein Meer aus Gedanken.

Es wird dunkler und dunkler,
schwerer und schwerer
drückt - die Last des Gedanken Meeres.

Und da geschieht es,
ich gehe verloren
verloren - zwischen zwei Gedanken.

Ertrinke zwischen Worten,
die mich mitreißen
mitreißen - in mein selbst erschaffenes Meer.

Und als ich wieder auftauche,
finde ich mich
- wieder.

Finde mich wieder,
und fühle mich
- endlich.

Endlich fühle ich mich,
und die Gedanken -
sind weg.

Sie gingen mir verloren,
als ich mich fühlte -
und fand.

Und jetzt
fühle und fühle ich,
und es wird
heller und heller.

Im Gedanken Meer.

is eternity infinite

infinite is the same as eternal, isn't it?

infinity means without ending
but with focus on an not wanted ending
bringing the ending right up to mind

eternity means for ever
with focus on the ever ongoing
wasting no thought to what's not wanted

so they are alike
but not quite the same.

eternity can be infinite
but infinity needn't be eternal.

thunderstorms

I really do love thunderstorms.

The smell of the rain.
The windy cold air.
The sound of thunder.

The magical lightning
brightening up everything
just for seconds.

It feels like the sky crashing for a moment.
Just shatter for this short instant.
Tearing everything apart.

And connecting everything at the same time.
It feels like cleansing.
Healing.
Getting one again.

In this wonder of nature, I feel peace.
Calming down.
Feeling my inner core.
like you've never done anything else.

Lichterketten und Sterne

Kleine glitzernde Punkte.
So weit entfernt, wie ein Winken.
Schillernd. Funkelnd.
Sterne.

Warmes weiches Scheinen.
Eine Handbreit weg, wie eine Umarmung.
Leuchtend. Strahlend.
Lichterkette.

Lichterketten sind Sterne zum Greifen.

the ocean sky

take a look at the
ocean.
it seems to be limitless,
like there's no ending.

take a look at the
sky.
it seems to be boundless,
like there's no beginning.

take a look at
both.
it seems as they
float into each other.

so when
ocean and sky
have no
limits

why should you?

Von Leer-Räumen
und Lehr-Räumen

Manchmal brauchen wir Leer-Räume für
Lehr-Räume.

Leer-Räume werden zu Lehr-Räumen,
wenn sie uns lehren den Raum zu leeren
und neuen Raum –
einzunehmen.

Doch wie füllen wir den leeren Raum,
machen wir ihn selbst zum Lehr-Raum
oder lehrt uns der Raum –
selbst.

Doch egal wie sehr wir ihn füllen wollen,
am Ende bleibt der Traum vom Lehr-Raum
nur ein leerer Traum ohne Raum,
weil wir uns verloren haben
in der Frage der –
Traumerfüllung.

Und packen wir die Fülle der leeren Träume
in den leeren Raum,
so wird der Leer-Raum gefüllt
und wandelt sich von selbst zum Lehr-Raum,
um zu lehren wie Traumleere
Räume füllt und Träume –
Erfüllt.

Ja, manchmal brauchen wir Leer-Räume für
Lehr-Räume.

beginnings

how can you be
sad about the sunset?

for you it's just
the end
of the day.

but for half of the
people on earth it's
the begin
of a new day.

so, there is no
ending
at all.

just a new
beginning
every day.

Bist du glücklich?

Hat dich schon mal jemand gefragt:
Bist du glücklich?

Aber wer zur Hölle ist denn dieser lich?
Dieser Lich von dem alle sprechen,
der der Bote des Glücks sein muss,
denn wird das Glück nicht meist mit ihm
im selben Atemzug genannt?

Sollte die Frage von jemandem nicht viel eher
lauten:
Bist du glückdich?

Bist du verbunden mit dem Glück,
steht es vor dir und begleitet es dich
durch deinen Tag, ja dein Leben?

Und was, wenn wir noch einen Schritt weiter
gehen?
Stelle ich mir selbst dann nicht besser die Frage:
Bin ich glückmich?

Begrüße ich das Glück herzlich,
wenn es vor mir steht
und lade es ein, mich zu begleiten?

Heißt es nun:
Bist du glückdich?
Bin ich glückmich?
Sind wir dann glücklich?

This is for You

An acceptance as limitless as it's possible.
A candidness as wide as an ocean deep.
A safety as strong as in a family.
A gratitude as big as it's for staying alive.
A closeness as near as there aren't miles apart.
A love as pure as nothing contrary exists.
A faith in each other as unconditional as it
should be.
A connection as deep as it seems it lasts since a
lifetime.